Hello friends?

Are you ready for an adventure?

In this special book, we will explore the amazing stories and teachings of Jesus. Get ready to color, learn, and discover how Jesus' love makes the world a more wonderful place. Let's begin our journey together!

Tereza Cristina

Today we will learn about a very special man named Jesus. He was very kind and helped everyone around him.

Color the picture of Jesus and the children.
Choose colors that you like!

Jesus was born in a place called Bethlehem. He came into the world on a peaceful night, bringing joy and hope to everyone who met him.

Color the stable and the star. You can use bright colors for the star and soft colors for the stable

A bright star appeared in the sky to show where Jesus was. This star guided the shepherds and kings to see the baby, showing how special Jesus was.

Color the star and the shepherds. Make the star shine with bright colors!

One special day, Jesus performed a miracle with five loaves and two fishes. He turned them into enough food to feed a large crowd, showing how important it is to share.

Color the food and the people. Try using lots of colors to show that it's a big celebration!

Jesus loved being with children. He knew that everyone, big and small, has a special place in God's heart.

Color Jesus and the children. Choose cheerful colors to show how happy everyone is.

Jesus taught that forgiveness is essential for living in peace. Even when someone does something wrong, forgiveness helps us move forward and maintain hope.

Color the embrace of Jesus and the symbols of forgiveness and hope. Use colors that convey warmth and tranquility

Jesus loved everyone with infinite love. He loved us so much that he gave His life for us. Jesus teaches us to be like him:
loving, kind, and ready to help others.

Color the scene of Jesus' love and the people helping each other. Choose colors that show how Jesus' love makes the world shine

Jesus' Special Love for Everyone

As Jesus grew, He showed His love in everything He did. Jesus didn't just love a few people—He loved everyone! He loved His friends, His family, and even strangers He had never met. His love was like a big, soft blanket that made everyone feel safe and warm.

Whenever Jesus saw someone who was sad or lonely, He would smile at them. His smile was like sunshine breaking through the clouds, making everyone feel better. Jesus' love was so strong that it could calm even the biggest worries—like when you're scared of the dark, but then someone turns on a gentle light, and suddenly, everything feels okay.

The Miracle of Sharing

One day, a huge crowd gathered to listen to Jesus. They were all hungry, but there wasn't enough food for everyone. Jesus noticed this and wanted to help. A little boy had five small loaves of bread and two fish—just enough for his own meal. But the boy was kind and shared his food with Jesus.

Jesus smiled, and something amazing happened! He took the bread and fish and turned them into enough food to feed the entire crowd. Everyone ate until they were full. This miracle wasn't just about the food—it was about love. Jesus showed that when we share, love grows. It's like when you share your favorite toy with a friend; the happiness doubles, and suddenly, both of you feel closer.

Jesus and the Children

Jesus loved spending time with children. He knew they had big hearts and important thoughts, just like grown-ups. When children came to see Jesus, He would kneel down to be on their level, so they could see the kindness in His eyes. His voice was always soft and calming, like a gentle breeze on a warm day.

Jesus taught that children are very special to God. He would often say, "Let the little children come to me, for the kingdom of heaven belongs to them." This meant that children are full of pure love—just like God's love for us.

The Power of Forgiveness

One of Jesus' most important lessons was about forgiveness. Sometimes, people do things that hurt our feelings, and it can make us feel upset. But Jesus taught that forgiveness is like cleaning up a mess. When you forgive someone, it's like wiping away all the hurt, so you can feel better inside. It doesn't mean you forget what happened, but it helps heal your little heart, so you can feel light and happy again.

Think of it like this: when you accidentally spill juice on the floor, at first, it feels like a big problem. But when you clean it up, the floor is shiny again, and you can move on. Forgiveness is like that—it cleans up the feelings, so we can move forward with peace in our hearts.

Love Without End

Jesus loved everyone with a love that never stops. His love is like a river that flows forever, always moving, always giving life. Jesus' love is with us even when we can't see Him. It's like the wind—you can't see the wind, but you can feel it. You can feel Jesus' love when you are kind to others, when you help a friend, or when someone is kind to you. It's always there, wrapping around you like a soft hug.

One day, Jesus gave the ultimate act of love: He gave His life for us. But even though He left the world for a while, His love never left. It stayed with us, growing inside our hearts, so we can share it with everyone we meet. Every time you show kindness, you are sharing a piece of Jesus' love.

What Jesus Teaches Us

Jesus teaches us that love is not just a feeling—it's something we do.
When you help someone who is sad, when you listen to a friend, or when you say something kind, you are spreading love, just like Jesus did.

Imagine that love is like a candle. When you light someone else's candle with yours, your flame doesn't get smaller—it spreads, making the world a brighter place. Jesus wants us to be little candles, spreading light wherever we go.

Let's Remember

As we color, learn, and discover together in this book, remember that Jesus' love is always with us. When we share, forgive, and help others, we are showing the world what His love looks like. And just like the bright star that shined when Jesus was born, we can be bright stars in the world, lighting the way with love.

NOW LET'S COLOR SOME ANIMALS

THEY ARE AMAZING CREATURES THAT ALSO SHOW LOVE AND KINDNESS IN DIFFERENT WAYS."

Choose your favorite colors and bring these animals to life. Think about how each animal can be special and how you can show love and kindness like they do.

TURTLE

Here is the turtle, known for its patience and perseverance. Let's color the turtle and think about how we can be patient and persistent in our challenges.

15

ELEPHANT

The elephant is a large and gentle animal, known for its memory and care for family. Let's color the elephant and remember how important it is to care for and remember our friends and family.

16

MONKEY

The monkey loves to play and have fun. Let's color the monkey and think of ways to bring joy and fun into our lives and the lives of those around us.

17

LION CUB

The lion cub is brave and loves to explore. Let's color the cub and remember how courage helps us explore and face new challenges.

PENGUIN

The penguin lives in a cold environment but is very friendly and protective. Let's color the penguin and think about how we can be friends and protect those we love.

GIRAFFE

The giraffe has a long neck that helps it reach high leaves. Let's color the giraffe and remember how patience and perseverance help us reach our goals.

20

BEAR

The bear is a strong and protective animal. Let's color the bear and think about how we can be strong and protect our friends and family.

21

RABBIT

The rabbit is quick and loves to hop. Let's color the rabbit and remember how it's important to be active and enjoy moments of fun.

22

HORSE

The horse runs swiftly and enjoys playing in the field. Let's color the horse and think about how strength and playfulness make life joyful and fun.

BIRD

The bird sings sweetly and enjoys flying in the sky. Let's color the bird and imagine how music and freedom make the world a beautiful place.

24

OWL

The owl is wise and watches over the night. Let's color the owl and think about how wisdom and careful observation can help us understand and learn more about the world.

25

DOLPHIN

The dolphin is intelligent and loves to play in the water. Let's color the dolphin and think about how intelligence and joy can make life more enjoyable.

26

FISH

The fish swims gracefully and loves to explore the water. Let's color the fish and think about how exploration and freedom make life exciting.

DOG

The dog is known for its loyalty and friendship. Let's color the dog and remember how loyalty and friendship are important in our lives

28

TIPS FOR PARENTS AND EDUCATORS

This book is designed to help children understand Jesus' teachings in a fun and accessible way. We adapted the book for children with autism and ADHD, and used a special font to make reading easier for children with dyslexia. Dyslexia is a condition that makes reading and writing challenging, but with tools and adaptations, everyone can learn and have fun. Here are some tips

- ✓ Talk about the illustrations while the child colors
- ✓ Use the activities to reinforce Jesus' teachings
- ✓ Encourage the child to share what they have learned with others
- ✓ For children with dyslexia, read the text aloud and help the child follow the words

Thank you for exploring the stories of Jesus with us!
We hope you had fun and learned a lot about love and kindness.
Remember, just as Jesus taught, you can also spread love and make a difference in the world. Keep coloring and sharing joy with everyone around you!

By

TEREZA CRISTINA

For more information about the book and other projects, visit your email
terezaaguilar.marketing@gmail.com

© 2024 Tereza C. de Aguilar Goncalves All rights reserved. No part of this book may be reproduced or transmitted in any form or by any means without permission